THE COMPLETE LOW CARB COOKBOOK

© **Copyright 2018 by Charlie Mason - All rights reserved.**

The following Book is reproduced below with the goal of providing information that is as accurate and reliable as possible. Regardless, purchasing this Book can be seen as consent to the fact that both the publisher and the author of this book are in no way experts on the topics discussed within and that any recommendations or suggestions that are made herein are for entertainment purposes only. Professionals should be consulted as needed prior to undertaking any of the action endorsed herein.

This declaration is deemed fair and valid by both the American Bar Association and the Committee of Publishers Association and is legally binding throughout the United States.

Furthermore, the transmission, duplication or reproduction of any of the following work including specific information will be considered an illegal act irrespective of if it is d1 electronically or in print. This extends to creating a secondary or tertiary copy of the work or a recorded copy and is only allowed with express written consent from the Publisher. All additional rights reserved.

The information in the following pages is broadly considered to be a truthful and accurate account of facts and as such any inattention, use or misuse of the information in question by the reader will render any resulting actions solely under their purview. There are no scenarios in which the publisher or the original author of this work can be in any fashion deemed liable for any hardship or damages that may befall them after undertaking information described herein.

Additionally, the information in the following pages is intended only for informational purposes and should thus be thought of as universal. As befitting its nature, it is presented without assurance regarding its prolonged validity or interim quality. Trademarks that are menti1d are d1 without written consent and can in no way be considered an endorsement from the trademark holder.

Table of Contents

CHAPTER ONE: BREAKFAST RECIPES 4
- Cheesy Flipped Egg 4
- Low Carb Eggs and Vegetables 6
- One Cup Frittata 7
- Low Carb Italian Breakfast Casserole 8
- Fabulous Low Carb Oat Meal 10
- Low Carb Pancakes 12
- Hash Brown Potato Cakes 14

CHAPTER TWO: LUNCH RECIPES 16
- Chicken Salad Stuffed Avocados 16
- Easy Shrimp Cobb Salad 18
- Chicken Curry Cup of Noodles 19
- Chicken, Charred Tomato, and Broccoli Salad 21
- Low Carb Burgers 23

CHAPTER THREE: DINNER RECIPES 25
- Chicken Wings with Greens 25
- Roasted Pork Belly Bites with Braised Cabbage 26
- Slow Cooker Chile with Cauliflower Rice 28
- Slow Cooker Beef Burritos 30
- Chipotle Steak Bowl 32
- Guacamole Sauce 33
- Keto Meat Pie 34

CHAPTER FOUR: LOW CARB DESSERTS 36
- Cream Cheese Tart Shells 36
- No-Bake Chocolate Swirl Delight 37
- Low Carb, Gluten Free Shortbread Cookies 39

As a way of saying thank you for purchasing my book, please use your link below to claim your 3 FREE Cookbooks on Health, Fitness & Dieting Instantly

https://bit.ly/2v8hWhk

You can also share your link with your friends and families whom you think that can benefit from the cookbooks or you can forward them the link as a gift!

CHAPTER ONE

BREAKFAST RECIPES

Breakfast is the most important meal of the day. So let's get started with some great recipes to get you and your family on their way. Some of these recipes can be done ahead of time and cooked on the fly, making them perfect for the busy family. They feed the family and still Mom out of the kitchen in time to go about her busy day. Some of these recipes are also kid-friendly, allowing your children to get involved in preparing the meal. Most of them can also be eaten any time of the day, making them a great way to stick with your low carb lifestyle and involve the family in their preparation.

Cheesy Flipped Egg

This one is quick and easy, and the kids just love it. It's a great way to fuel them before they out the door to face their day. In fact, it's a great one for the parents, too:

Ingredients:
- Butter, 1 tablespoon
- Cheddar cheese (unprocessed), 1 slice
- Double (or heavy) cream, 2 tablespoons
- Egg, 1 beaten

What to Do:
1. Heat the butter in a small fry pan over moderate heat.
2. Using a small dish, mix the heavy cream and egg.

Chapter One: Breakfast Recipes

3. Pour the mixture into the skillet and let it cook until it starts to bubble up.
4. Flip the egg mixture over and add the slice of cheese.
5. Cook for about 10 seconds until the cheese the melts.

Serve with a slice of low carb toast and butter.

Low Carb Eggs and Vegetables

Let's face it, when someone thinks of breakfast, they think of only eggs. Not true, my friend. Add some veggies for a great "fuel-me" breakfast.

Ingredients:

- Coconut oil, two tablespoons, heated
- California Mix vegetables, frozen (you can make your own mix of frozen broccoli, cauliflower, onions and green beans, 1 cup of each)
- Spinach, one cup (optional, but suggested for nutrition)
- Salt and pepper to taste
- Eggs, four beaten

What to Do:

1. Place the vegetables in the oil and stir until cooked through.
2. Add the eggs and spices.
3. Stir frequently to finish cooking.
4. Serve as is or with a slice of low carb toast.

You can also make this dish for lunch or dinner.

Chapter One: Breakfast Recipes

One Cup Frittata

There are times that you want just a little something for yourself after the family has gone to school or work. This one fits the bill.

- Egg, one
- Bacon bits, two tablespoons
- Double cream (heavy cream), two tablespoons
- Green pepper, one quarter cup
- Cheddar Cheese, one quarter cup

What to Do:

1. Mix the above ingredients in a large mug that has been sprayed with cooking oil.
2. Put it in the microwave and cook for one and half minutes.
3. If desired, you can add more cheese.

You might want a spoon for this one since you'll want every bite!

Low Carb Italian Breakfast Casserole

You can make this recipe ahead of time and simply heat it in your microwave for a great tasting, nutritious breakfast on the go.

Ingredients:

- Italian sausage, twelve ounces
- Cauliflower, seven ounces, cut into bite-sized pieces and rinsed
- Butter, two ounces
- Eggs, eight, slightly beaten
- Heavy cream (Double cream), one cup
- Fresh Basil, four tablespoons, chopped (You can also use two tablespoons dried basil.)
- Shredded cheese of your choice, five ounces
- Pepper and seasoning salt to taste

What to Do:

1. Heat your oven to 200 degrees Celsius (400 degrees Fahrenheit)
2. Rinse and trim the cauliflower. Cut into bite-size pieces
3. Add butter to a skillet and fry the cauliflower until it starts to soften
4. Add sausage to the pan and crumble as it cooks thoroughly and the mix is golden brown.
5. Sprinkle with a little pepper and seasoning salt.
6. Grease a baking dish and pour in the sausage mix

7. Using a medium mixing bowl, combine the remaining ingredients except for the basil
8. Add the eggs to the sausage mix. Add the basil on top.
9. Let the mix cook for 30 to 40 minutes or until the mix is set and turns golden brown.

If the casserole is not set yet but shows signs that it could burn, you can cover the dish with a sheet of aluminum foil. When done, let it cool for about ten minutes before serving.

If made beforehand, you can heat each serving of the casserole in the microwave for two minutes before serving.

The Complete Low Carb Cookbook

Fabulous Low Carb Oat Meal

Alright, this one does not contain oats. But you won't miss them with this great recipe. You can also make this one ahead of time, and cook as you need it.

Ingredients:
- Chia seeds, one tablespoon.
- Flaxseed, one tablespoon.
- Almond or coconut milk, one cup.
- Sunflower seeds (no shells), one tablespoon.
- Salt, a pinch if desired.

What to Do:
1. Add all of the ingredients to a small saucepan. Bring it to a boil.
2. Turn the heat down and let it simmer until it reaches your desired thickness. (This shouldn't take more than a couple of minutes.) Stir well.
3. Top with butter and either almond or coconut milk.

Some tips on this one: You can add a touch of cinnamon, fresh fruit, raisins or nuts. You're only limited by your imagination.

Here is the recipe to store some for later:
- Flaxseed, one and one-quarter cups.
- Chia seeds, one and one-quarter cups.
- Sunflower seeds (no shells), one and one-quarter cups.
- Cinnamon, one tablespoon.
- Salt, one-half teaspoon (optional).

Chapter One: Breakfast Recipes

Mix the above ingredients and store in a sealed container. To use, measure three tablespoons of the seed mixture to one cup of almond or coconut milk for a quick breakfast. Cook as instructed or for two minutes in the microwave. Stir and cook thirty seconds longer each time until desired thickness is obtained.

Low Carb Pancakes

This one is a recipe that will cure that craving for pancakes in the morning. Not only are they nutritious, but they cure that urge to have fried foods that you shouldn't have.

There is also a do-ahead tip on this one: Mix the ingredients and store in the refrigerator. In the morning, simply put the oil in the pan and start cooking.

Ingredients:

- Eggs, two, beaten.
- Pork rinds, two-thirds ounces, finely crushed.
- Cashew, almond or coconut milk, two tablespoons. (Make sure they are unsweetened.)
- Ground cinnamon, one teaspoon.
- Maple extract, one teaspoon.
- Coconut oil, two tablespoons.

What to Do:

1. Add the pork rinds to a blender and use a pulse setting until the rinds are reduced to a fine powder.
2. Add the remaining ingredients and combine them until smooth.
3. Using a tablespoon of oil, place a skillet on moderate heat.
4. Add one-quarter cup of the batter to pan and brown. Flip the pancake to brown on the other side. It takes about two minutes before you flip it.
5. Remove the cooked pancake to a plate. Continue cooking the batter as described.

Chapter One: Breakfast Recipes

To serve, you can add a dollop of sour cream, fresh fruit or browned butter. (As a personal note, I eat these with my home-canned peaches, pears or apples on the side. Just be sure they are canned with no refined sugar.)

Hash Brown Potato Cakes

You don't have to deprive yourself of some of the great foods in the world. Potatoes are one of the biggest ones on the craving list. This recipe cures that in a low carb way. But you have to remember that moderation is the key to any diet. This doesn't mean that you can't indulge in great food. It simply means that you, and only you, have control over what you eat. However, you should indulge in a good recipe that is both low carb and diabetic friendly.

Ingredients:

- Onion, one-half, thinly sliced and chopped.
- Olive oil, one tablespoon.
- Shredded hash brown potatoes, one pound.
- Thyme, two teaspoons of fresh, snipped, or one-quarter teaspoon dried.
- Salt, one-quarter teaspoon.
- Black pepper, one-eighth teaspoon.
- Cooking spray.

What to Do:

1. Using a 300-degree setting, turn your oven on.
2. Spray a bit of cooking spray into a skillet. Place on medium heat while you make the mix.
3. Combine the first six ingredients in a large bowl.
4. Make a potato patty and place into the heated pan using a rounded tablespoon of the mix. Flatten the patty down as it cooks for five minutes. Very carefully turn

the patty over to brown on the other side for another five minutes. They should be golden brown when done.

5. Place the patties on a baking sheet and put them in the oven to stay warm while you fry the rest of the patties. Use more cooking spray as necessary to fry.
6. When you have finished frying the patties, leave all to heat for five to ten minutes in the oven.

Serve the patties warm. You can also warm them up as leftover using your microwave in a two-minute setting.

CHAPTER TWO

LUNCH RECIPES

In today's world, lunch is usually eaten at work or on the run as you do your errands. So it goes without saying that it has to be portable, easy to fix and nutritious. The last thing you want to do on a low carb diet is head to the nearest fast food place!

Chicken Salad Stuffed Avocados

This is a make-ahead recipe that you can carry to work with you for your midday meal. Not only is it low carb, but it is a taste treat that will get you through your afternoon on a busy day.

Ingredients:

- Plain, low-fat Greek yogurt, one-third cup.
- Mayonnaise (not salad dressing), one-quarter cup.
- Tarragon, one tablespoon chopped fresh or one teaspoon dried.
- Salt, three-quarters of a teaspoon.
- Ground pepper, one-quarter teaspoon.
- Celery, chopped, one cup.
- Boneless, skinless chicken breast, one pound.
- Seedless red grapes, one cup, halved if desired.
- Toasted chopped pecans, one-quarter cup.
- Avocados, two firm and ripe, halved and pitted.

Chapter Two: Lunch Recipes

What to Do:

1. Using a large saucepan, add the chicken. Pour in enough water to cover the meat. Boil until done, about 15 minutes. (You can also use canned chicken, but be careful of the sodium content.)
2. Chop or shred slightly cooled chicken and refrigerate until thoroughly cooled about 30 minutes.
3. Place the yogurt, mayonnaise, tarragon, pepper, and salt into a sizable bowl. Stir until well combined.
4. Add the chicken, celery, grapes, and pecans. Stir until combined.
5. At this point, you can refrigerate the salad to use later. (It will keep up to three days refrigerated.) To serve it, fill each avocado half with about one-half cup of the salad. Serve immediately or place in a container to take with you.

Just a note: If you're storing the salad for later use, do not store it with the avocado. Fill the avocado just before serving for the best result.

Easy Shrimp Cobb Salad

This is an easy salad that can be tossed together ahead of time for a satisfying lunch. While not heavy in calories, it is on protein.

Ingredients:

- Boneless, skinless chicken breast, one pound.
- Romaine lettuce, three cups, chopped.
- Cherry or grape tomatoes, five.
- Cucumber, sliced, one-quarter cup (slightly more if desired).
- Hard-boiled egg, one, sliced.
- Large shrimp, five, cooked and peeled with tails removed.
- Freshly ground pepper to taste.
- Light blue cheese dressing, two tablespoons.

What to Do:

1. To hard-boil the eggs, place them in a single layer in the bottom of a saucepan. Add enough water to cover the eggs. Bring to a boil. Turn the heat down to a simmer for ten minutes. Remove from heat, pour off the boiling water and place them under a constant stream of cold water until the eggs are cooled. (This makes them easier to peel.) Refrigerate until ready to use.

2. Layer the salad ingredients, putting the sliced egg on top. If you're not serving the salad immediately, place the dressing in a separate container.

3. When ready to serve, pour the dressing over the top and stir gently to mix.

Chapter Two: Lunch Recipes

Chicken Curry Cup of Noodles

A busy lifestyle begs you to ask, "What's for lunch?" When you don't have much time, this lunchtime treat is a great one for people on the go. The prep is easy and is done ahead of time. When lunchtime rolls around, it's ready in two to three minutes.

This recipe makes three jars.

Ingredients:

- Chicken bouillon paste, 3 teaspoons, divided.
- Red curry paste, six teaspoons, divided.
- Coconut milk, six tablespoons, divided.
- Large shrimp, five, cooked and peeled with tails removed.
- Frozen stir-fry vegetables, one and one-half cups, divided.
- Chicken breast, nine ounces, cooked and chopped, divided.
- Spiralized zucchini noodles, one and one-half cups, divided.
- Cilantro, chopped, three tablespoons, divided.

What to Do:

1. Layer the divided ingredients into the bottom of three one and one-half pint jars. Cover and refrigerate.
2. When ready to prepare, add one cup of very hot water to a jar. Shake to mix well.

3. Remove the lid and place in the microwave in one-minute increments until steaming hot.
4. Let stand for five minutes before serving. (For more tender noodles, loosely set the lid back on the jar to hold some steam.)
5. Stir and eat!

Chapter Two: Lunch Recipes

Chicken, Charred Tomato, and Broccoli Salad

Since lunch is something that most of us do on the fly, it's best to prepare them ahead of time. Having a dish in the refrigerator to pull out on the run is a good way to be sure you're not turning to a fast food restaurant just to have something in your stomach.

This one only looks complicated on the surface. It's actually simple to make if you do the ingredients ahead of time and prepare a dish to go. Not only do you get rounded, low carb nutrition, but you save money by doing special orders at a restaurant. Besides, the waiting time at a restaurant for your special order cuts into the time you have to savor your food.

This recipe makes six servings. You can adjust it as needed, but if your whole family needs a great lunch, you will want to make the full recipe!

Ingredients:

- Broccoli florets, three cups.
- Tomatoes, one and one-half pounds, medium.
- Shredded, cooked chicken breast, three cups.
- Extra virgin olive oil, two teaspoons plus three tablespoons.
- Ground black pepper, one teaspoon.
- Chili powder, one-half teaspoon.
- Salt, one teaspoon.
- Lemon juice, one-quarter cup.

What to Do:

1. Boil a large pot of water and toss in the broccoli. Cook for about five minutes. Remove the hot water and pour in cold water until cooled. Drain well.

2. In the meantime, cut the tomatoes in half and squeeze them gently to remove the seeds.

3. Place the tomatoes on a paper towel (cut side down) to remove moisture for a few minutes.

4. Using a big, heavy skillet (I use an iron one), heat on a burner until sizzling hot. Coat the tomatoes with olive oil, and place in the pan cut side down. Cook until starting to char and soften, about three to five minutes.

5. Brush the tomatoes with oil again and turn to char the skins, about two minutes. Once charred, move the tomatoes a plate. (Leave the pan as it is!)

6. Pour the rest of the three tablespoons of olive oil to the pan and add the pepper, salt, and chili powder. Mix continuously for about forty-five seconds to cook. Remove the pan from heat. Scrape the pan to loosen the browned bits. Slowly pour in the lemon juice. Be careful of any splatter! Remove from heat and stir well.

7. Chop the tomatoes into large chunks and add to an adequately-sized bowl. Pour in the broccoli and chicken. Drizzle the pan drippings over the top.

You can cover and refrigerate this dish for up to two days. However, as good as it is, you won't have any to waste here. Lunch is served!

Chapter Two: Lunch Recipes

Low Carb Burgers

Every once in awhile we all crave a good burger, but we still want to maintain our low carb lifestyle. This burger does just that. You can have this for a lunch or during a Barbeque. Just take your fixings with you and slap your burger on the grill.

Ingredients:

- Garlic powder, one-half teaspoon.
- Soy sauce, one and one-half tablespoons.
- Egg, one, slightly beaten.
- Onion, one small, well minced.
- Turkey, beef, chicken or pork, ground, one and one-half pounds.
- Low carb bread, twelve slices.

What to Do:

1. Mix all ingredients together, except the bread. Be sure they are mixed well.
2. Press into six patties. If you like thicker burgers, press accordingly and decrease the number of low carb bread slices you will need.
3. Brown in a pan with a small amount of coconut oil, or put them on the grill to brown. Just be sure the inner temperature of the burgers reaches 160 degrees for safe eating.
4. Place each burger patty on one slice of low carb bread.
5. Add the condiments you would like, making sure that they do not contain refined sugar. Catsup or Ketchup can contain sugar. Mustard is usually sugar-free.

The Complete Low Carb Cookbook

Relish sometimes contains sugar. If preferred, you can moisten your burger with a slice of cheese instead. Usually, they do not contain sugar.

6. Enjoy your low carb burger with your friends or family. And remember, you're living a great lifestyle in nutrition.

If your friends and family know that you live a low carb lifestyle, they will not be offended when you bring your own burger to their barbeque. But if you are faced with a situation, eat only the meat. That's usually your best bet.

CHAPTER THREE

DINNER RECIPES

Dinner is the meal where the family can be together and share a great meal over discussion of the events of the day. You want something fulfilling while being low carb, too. Skimping on flavor and nutrition is not an option. So here are some great ones to try.

Chicken Wings with Greens

This is another recipe that is variable, depending on the people you have to feed. You can add or decrease as needed.

Ingredients:

- Spinach greens or lettuce leaves.
- Chicken wings, tips cut off and rinsed. Plan two to four for each person.
- Spices as desired. (There is a spice mix you can get commercially or mix your own as desired.)

What to Do:

1. Heat your oven to a 350-degree setting.
2. Rinse the chicken wings and put them between paper towels to dry off a bit.
3. Coat the chicken with the desired spices.
4. Place a sheet of aluminum foil over a sheet pan and douse it with cook spray.
5. Put the spiced chicken on the pan in a single layer.
6. Bake for 45 minutes or until they are browned.
7. Serve with spinach or lettuce leaves for a great meal.

Roasted Pork Belly Bites with Braised Cabbage

This recipe is easy to do and has a lot of flavors. One caveat, though: If you are a calorie counter, you might want to adjust the portions accordingly. Each plate dinner has about 900 calories per serving. But in the low carb world, calorie counting is not usually part of the equation.

Pork Belly Bites

Ingredients:

- Salt and pepper to taste.
- Fennel seeds, two teaspoons.
- Olive oil, two tablespoons.
- Pork belly, two pounds.

Braised Cabbage

- White cabbage (or Savoy cabbage), one-quarter of a head, finely shredded.
- Cloves, two.
- Olive oil, two tablespoons.
- Anise, one star.
- Caraway seeds, two teaspoons.
- Red cabbage, one-quarter of head, finely shredded.
- Red wine vinegar, two tablespoons.
- Chicken stock, one cup.

What to Do:

- Preheat your oven to 425 degrees.

Chapter Three: Dinner Recipes

- Score the pig belly skin with a sharp knife, creating one-inch strips. Do not cut into the meat. Rub the entire pork belly with the oil, fennel seeds, salt, and pepper. Make sure the seasonings get into scores you made.
- Place the pork belly on a baking pan, skin side up. Put in the oven and let cook for 20 minutes, so that the skin just starts to get crispy.
- Reduce the oven temperature to 325 degrees and bake the pork for one and one-half to two hours or until the pork is tender.
- While the pork is baking, pour the oil in a fairly big sauté pan and heat over medium heat.
- Put in the cloves, anise, and caraway seeds and cook so that they are popping slightly.
- Add the cabbage to the pan with a generous pinch of salt. Stir to coat the cabbage and cook gently for about five minutes until the cabbage begins to soften.
- While the cabbage is still cooking, turn the oven back up to 425 degrees. Cook the pork for about twenty minutes more, or until the skin is nice and crispy. Take out of the oven and let cool for about fifteen minutes.
- While the pork bakes, add the chicken stock to the cabbage and simmer for another ten minutes to be sure the cabbage is done. Take the pan off the heat and drain any excess stock. Add the vinegar and stir well.
- Using the scores you made in the pork belly, cut the pork into chunks. Serve with the Braised cabbage on the side.

If desired, you can still add a side salad, although it isn't necessary.

Slow Cooker Chile with Cauliflower Rice

This is a recipe that you put in your slow cooker, and go about your business whatever it may be. When the meal is ready, you can sit down to a great meal with very little effort put into it. Not only is it nutritious and low carb, but is also a comforting meal on a cold day. You can serve a good hot meal to six people with this recipe.

Ingredients:

- Cauliflower, one large head.
- Olive oil, one tablespoon.
- Pork sausage, one pound.
- Ground beef, 80% lean, one pound.
- Olive oil, one tablespoon.
- Yellow onion, one small, diced.
- Green peppers, two small, diced.
- Tomatoes, two cups, diced.
- Chili powder, two tablespoons.
- Cumin, one teaspoon.
- Water, one-quarter cup.
- Pepper and salt as desired.

What to Do:

- Brown the sausage and beef in a skillet. Drain off the fat.
- Place the meat mixture in the slow cooker, layering it into the bottom.

Chapter Three: Dinner Recipes

- Add the onion, peppers, tomatoes, cumin, chili powder and water. Add salt and pepper as desired.
- Stir the contents and cover. Cook on low heat for six to eight hours, stirring occasionally.
- While the chili is cooking, place the cleaned cauliflower florets in a blender. Pulse into rice-like grains.
- Pour the olive oil into a sizable sauté pan and place over heat. Put the cauliflower "grains" in and cook so that they are tender, about five to eight minutes.
- Serve the chili and cauliflower separated on a plate. You can add green chilis and fresh cut green onions if you like.
- While eating, mix some of the cauliflower with each bite of chili. Enjoy!

Slow Cooker Beef Burritos

Any day of the week can be a busy one. That doesn't mean that you can't prepare a satisfying meal for the family to enjoy for dinner. This is one that is not only easy to prepare ahead of time but one that your family will have fun putting together for each burrito. This recipe feeds four. You can multiply it as needed.

Slow Cooker Beef

Ingredients:

- Garlic powder, two teaspoons.
- Garlic cloves, four minced.
- Black pepper, one-half teaspoon.
- Sea salt, two teaspoons.
- Cinnamon, one teaspoon.
- Ground chipotle pepper, one teaspoon, optional.
- White onion, one-half, coarsely chopped.
- Chicken broth, one cup.
- Bay leaves, two.
- Top Sirloin steak, rinsed, patted dry and scored on all sides.
- Low carb barbeque sauce, one cup.
- Low carb wraps, eight.
- Coleslaw mix, as much as needed for the burritos you plan. Recommended is about one and one-half cups for this recipe. (Usually, a bag from your grocery store with the rest being made into a salad later.)

Chapter Three: Dinner Recipes

- Mayonnaise,

What to Do:

1. Combine all of the spices and rub into the meat, being sure the spices get into the cuts you made.
2. Add the garlic and onion to the slow cooker first. Put the steak in next and pour in the chicken broth. Place the bay leaves into the broth. Cook for eight hours on low.
3. When the steak is finished cooking, remove it to a plate. Drain the liquid out of the pot and remove the bay leaves. Leave the onion and garlic or place it on the plate with the steak. Shred the steak and add all back to the pot.
4. Add the cup of barbeque sauce and stir well.
5. To assemble the burritos, add some of the slow cooker beef to a tortilla, toss on a small bit of the coleslaw mix and top with mayonnaise. Roll the tortilla, tucking one end.

No additions are needed for this meal, but you can also add mushrooms to the steak mix or put a salad on the side.

Chipotle Steak Bowl

This is another tasty treat for dinner that is guilt-free. You can use any meat you want in it: Pork, chicken, ground beef or even tuna, if that's your style. However you make it, it will still be delicious!

It uses a homemade Guacamole sauce, so it is included for your reference after the main recipe.

Ingredients:

- Salt and pepper, as desired.
- Skirt steak, one pound.
- Homemade Guacamole sauce, one recipe.
- Pepper Jack cheese, four ounces.
- Sour cream, one cup.
- Fresh cilantro, about one handful.
- Chipotle Tabasco sauce, just a splash or two.

What to Do:

1. Season the meat with pepper and salt to your taste.
2. Heat a skillet over high heat. Cook the meat for about three to four minutes on each side. Remove to a plate.
3. Prepare your guacamole.
4. Slice the steak into thin, bite-sized strips, dividing it into four portions.
5. Shred the cheese, and top the four portions with it.
6. Add about one-quarter cup of guacamole and one-quarter cup of sour cream to each portion.
7. If desired, splash each portion with a dash of Chipotle Tabasco sauce and a bit of fresh cut cilantro. Dinner is served!

Chapter Three: Dinner Recipes

Guacamole Sauce

Ingredients:

- Red onion, one-quarter cup, diced fine.
- Grape tomatoes, six, diced fine.
- Garlic, one close squeezed or one eight teaspoons of powder.
- Olive oil, one tablespoon.
- Cilantro, one tablespoon, chopped fine.
- Salt, one-quarter teaspoon.
- Pepper, one-eighth teaspoon.
- Crushed red pepper, one-eighth teaspoon. (Optional)
- Avocados, two, pitted, cut and mashed.

What to Do:

1. Add the ingredients in order as listed.
2. Stir well and enjoy! You can also make this one to dip pork rinds or low carb crackers as a snack.

Keto Meat Pie

This is another versatile recipe that can use any meat. Not only is nutritious and low carb, but it is also a comfort food to fuel you during your wind-down and sleep time. It is fulfilling and delicious, as well as being rather easy.

Filling:

Ingredients:

- Yellow onion, one-half, chopped.
- Garlic clove, one, finely chopped.
- Butter or olive oil, two tablespoons.
- Ground lamb or beef, one and one-third pounds.
- Salt and pepper to taste.
- Dried oregano or basil, one tablespoon.
- Tomato paste, four tablespoons.
- Water, one-half cup.

Pie Crust

- Sesame seeds, four tablespoons.
- Coconut flour, four tablespoons.
- Psyllium husk powder, one tablespoon.
- Baking powder, one teaspoon.
- Salt, just a pinch.
- Olive or coconut oil, three tablespoons.
- Egg, one, slightly beaten.
- Water, four tablespoons.

Topping:
- Cottage cheese, eight ounces.
- Shredded cheese of your choice, seven ounces.

Instructions:
1. Preheat your oven to 350 degrees.
2. Cook the onion and garlic in a bit of coconut oil or butter until translucent and fragrant.
3. Add the meat and cook until browned. Sprinkle the basil or oregano, pepper, and salt while cooking for the flavors to mix.
4. Drain the meat. Add the pesto and water. Continue to simmer for about twenty minutes.
5. While the meat is cooking, make the crust for the pie.
6. Mix all of the ingredients for the crust in a food processor until it forms a ball. If you don't have a food processor, you can mix it with a fork and knead it a bit until the ingredients are thoroughly mixed.
7. Grease a nine-inch or 10-inch pie pan, and add a piece of circular-cut parchment paper to it. (This makes it easier to remove the pie when it's done.)
8. Spread your dough into the pan using well-oiled fingers or an oiled spatula.
9. Pre-bake the crust for about fifteen minutes. Make sure it begins to turn brown.
10. Remove crust from the oven and place the meat mixture in it.
11. Top with the cheese mix.
12. Place the pie in the oven and bake for thirty to forty minutes or until the pie is set well and the cheese is well browned. Let the pie set for fifteen minutes before cutting.
13. Serve each portion with a fresh green salad.

CHAPTER FOUR

LOW CARB DESSERTS

You would be missing out on life if you couldn't have dessert with a meal. A low carb lifestyle is no different. Just because you are limiting some things in your diet doesn't mean you have to miss out on a dessert or two. You can still have those. Cure your craving for sweets while limiting the sugars that convert to fat in your body.

Cream Cheese Tart Shells

This is another versatile recipe. Fill the shells with your favorite low carb filling, such as fresh fruits, sweet cheese or puddings.

Ingredients:

- Butter, one-half cup, softened.
- Almond or coconut flour, one cup.
- Cream cheese, three ounces, softened.

What to Do:

1. Blend the cream cheese and butter.
2. Add the flour slowly, combining well as you go.
3. Chill the mixture for about an hour. (You can make this ahead and chill for a maximum of 24 hours.)
4. Heat your oven to a 325-degree setting.
5. Make 24 one-inch balls with the dough. Press the dough into one and one-half inch muffin cups to form a shallow shell.
6. Fill with your favorite filling and bake for twenty minutes or until the shell is nicely browned.

Chapter Four: Low Carb Desserts

No-Bake Chocolate Swirl Delight

This is definitely a sweet treat that satisfies. It's soft and creamy with enough chocolate to bring that feeling of euphoria.

Ingredients:

- Fat-free milk, three-quarters of a cup.
- Fat-free cream cheese, two eight-ounce packages.
- Unflavored gelatin, one envelope.
- Sugar substitute, equivalent to one-third cup of sugar.
- Sour cream, one eight-ounce carton.
- Semi-sweet chocolate chips, four ounces, melted and cooled.
- Vanilla, two teaspoons.

What to Do:

1. Using a small saucepan, pour in the milk.
2. Sprinkle the gelatin over the top and set aside for five minutes.
3. Stirring constantly over low heat make sure the gelatin is well incorporated.
4. Shut off the heat, stir and set aside for fifteen minutes.
5. In the meantime, whip the creamed cheese in a big bowl until creamed.
6. Add the sour cream. Blend well.
7. Stir in the sugar substitute, a small bit at a time while beating.
8. Gradually add the gelatin mixture. Blend well.

9. Divide the mixture into two equal parts.
10. Drizzle the melted chocolate into one-half while still blending.
11. Oil a spring-form pan. Put half of the chocolate mixture into the pan.
12. Put half of the white mixture over the chocolate mixture.
13. Swirl the two slightly with a narrow spatula or butter knife.
14. Add the remaining chocolate mixture topped by the remaining white mixture.
15. Swirl the two again.
16. Place foil or plastic wrap over the pan and refrigerate six hours, until thoroughly set.
17. To serve, gently loosen the cheese mixture from the sides of the pan. Remove the cheesy treat from the pan by removing the outer pan.
18. Cut into slices. You can also add chocolate curls as a garnish.

** Remember to use your link to claim your 3 FREE Cookbooks on Health, Fitness & Dieting Instantly

https://bit.ly/2v8hWhk

Chapter Four: Low Carb Desserts

Low Carb, Gluten Free Shortbread Cookies

This recipe has only five ingredients. Simple to do and makes a great sweet treat for snack time, too.

Ingredients:
- Almond flour, one and one-third cups.
- Sweetener, equivalent to one quarter cup.
- Vanilla, one-half teaspoon.
- Butter, one-quarter cup.
- Salt, one-eighth teaspoon.

What to Do:
1. Preheat your oven to 350 degrees. Using parchment paper, cover a cookie sheet and put off to the side.
2. Mix all ingredients well. It will form a crumble. Press together into a ball.
3. Refrigerate for about ten minutes.
4. Knead the ball and divide the ball into one teaspoon scoops. Form a ball of each one.
5. Place the balls on dough on the prepared baking pan leaving a bit of space between each one. Use a fork to slightly flatten the dough.
6. Bake until slightly browned on the edges, about eight to eleven minutes.
7. Remove to a rack or parchment paper to cool.
8. You can top these with chocolate drizzle or a fresh fruit mash.

You can also serve these with a tea or coffee clutch. Either plain or with fruit, they are sure to please.

Printed in Great Britain
by Amazon